Talk to the wo
with EuroTalk

WELCOME to our catalogue and the start of what we hope will be a language adventure.

More people learn languages with EuroTalk than with any other computer software and now our range covers more than 100 languages.

Our CD and DVD ROMs work because the EuroTalk method taps into the natural linguistic talent we are all born with.

And, because we believe in our products, we offer a money-back guarantee if you're not completely happy with one for any reason.

Your opinion about our discs is also very important to us, so please let us know what you think.

And, if you want to register your interest in a language not already covered, you can do so on our website. We do respond to popular demand.

Happy learning!

Richard Howeson
Richard Howeson

More than five million people have used our products including: The International Red Cross, The American Foreign Service, UNESCO, two European Governments, British Aerospace the US and British Armies.....

Welcome

Talk Now!

"This is an excitingly different language learning series. Talk Now! uses games and quizzes as a basis for making the learning process fun and relaxing.

There's no better way to teach an old dog new tricks and this fun element of the programme means that your fears are forgotten as you absorb words and phrases without even realising you are learning them".

PC Answers

The world's **biggest and best selling** range of **language learning** CD-ROMs

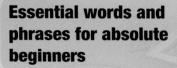

Essential words and phrases for absolute beginners

THIS is the world's best selling language learning CD-ROM series for beginners, used by more than three million people. Ideal for travellers, holidaymakers, business people, schoolchildren, students and families.

Special features include:
- Speech recording – compare your voice with native speakers.
- "Intelligent" software – remembers words you get wrong and targets your weak points.
- Four quiz levels – test what you've learnt.
- Automatic localisation – lets you choose the language you learn from (more than 100 available).

More than 100 languages

Available in 100+ languages: see map in centre pages for full list. But, as the number of new languages is growing all the time, check out our web site for the latest information.

Talk Now!

World Talk

World Talk language list:

- Afrikaans
- American English
- Arabic
- Cantonese
- Chinese Mandarin
- Czech
- Danish
- Dutch
- English
- French
- Finnish
- German
- Greek
- Hawaiian
- Hebrew
- Hindi
- Hungarian
- Icelandic
- Irish
- Italian
- Japanese
- Norwegian
- Polish
- Portuguese
- Russian
- Spanish
- Swedish
- Thai
- Turkish
- Welsh

Improve your **communication skills.**
It's a step up from our famous Talk Now!

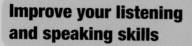

Improve your listening and speaking skills

IF you've mastered the basics in a language and want to improve your conversation, this CD-ROM is for you.

World Talk takes you to new levels with your language skills and gives you the confidence to chat with ease to native speakers.

The disc is for intermediate students and is a step up from our famous Talk Now! series.

Special features include:

- A TV-style quiz game in your chosen language. Challenge a friend to compete against you and see who is first on the buzzer with the right answer.
- A TV-style quiz game for one person in which you pit your language skills against a hilarious on-screen opponent. Watch him shake his head in despair if you win a point or punch the air in delight if he wins!
- Lots of 'real life' situations to test your comprehension and/or speech. e.g. you're given directions to the bank in your chosen language and then have to navigate your on-screen car to the correct destination.
- Speech recording and dictation writing practice.

World Talk

Movie Talk is available in...

English, French, German, Spanish, and Italian

English using the "Inspector Morse" movie, "Sins of the Father", French using "Au Coeur de la Loi", German using "Ein Fall Für Zwei", Spanish using "Querido Maestro" and Italian using "Mio Padre è Innocente".

Movie Talk is an **innovation** in language learning which gives you a **starring role** in a **big screen movie**.

Interactive Video language learning

Lights, camera, action...
Movie Talk DVD-ROM lets you learn a language as it's really spoken by taking you into the magical world of the big screen.

For advanced students, it's the next best thing to actually being in the country of your chosen language.

Using a hugely popular movie in your chosen language, the disc exploits the latest technology to help you speak like a local.

Special features let you:
- Take a starring role in the film by replacing one of the characters' voices with yours as the movie rolls.
- Choose your favourite scene and re-record it, giving yourself the best lines.
- Watch a video clip and score points if you can predict what the next character says.
- Listen to a video clip, then win points for correctly spelling what's been said.
- Play a TV-style quiz game in which you pit your language skills against an on-screen opponent.
- Choose whether or not to view the foreign language subtitles as the film rolls.
- Look up any words you don't know in one of two special picture dictionaries.

Movie Talk

Do we speak

1. **Afrikaans**
2. **Albanian**
3. **Alsatian**
4. **Amharic**
5. **American English**
6. **Arabic**
7. **Armenian**
8. **Assamese**
9. **Azeri**
10. **Basque**
11. **Bengali**
12. **Brazilian Portuguese**
13. **Breton**
14. **Burmese**
15. **Bulgarian**
16. **Catalan**
17. **Cantonese**
18. **Cockney**
19. **Cornish**
20. **Corsican**
21. **Croatian**
22. **Czech**
23. **Danish**
24. **Dutch**
25. **English**
26. **Estonian**
27. **Farsi**
28. **Finnish**
29. **French**
30. **Georgian**
31. **German**
32. **Greek**
33. **Gujarati**
34. **Hausa**
35. **Hawaiian**
36. **Hebrew**
37. **Hindi**
38. **Hungarian**
39. **Icelandic**
40. **Igbo**
41. **Indonesian**
42. **Inuktitut**
43. **Irish**
44. **Italian**
45. **Japanese**
46. **Jèrriais**
47. **Kannada**
48. **Kazakh**
49. **Khmer**
50. **Korean**
51. **Kurdish**
52. **Kyrgyz**
53. **Lao**
54. **Latin**

North & South America

Africa

All these languages are covered by our Talk Now! range with more being ad

our language?

55. Latvian
56. Lithuanian
57. Luxembourgisch
58. Macedonian
59. Malagasy
60. Malay
61. Malayalam
62. Mandarin
63. Maori
64. Marathi
65. Maltese
66. Manx
67. Mexican
    Spanish
68. Mongolian
69. Navajo
70. Nepali
71. Norwegian
72. Paplamento
73. Pashto
74. Pidgin
75. Punjabi
76. Polish
77. Portuguese
78. Quechua
79. Romanian
80. Romansch
81. Russian
82. Saami
83. Sardinian
84. Savo
85. Scots Gaelic
86. Serb
87. Setswana
88. Shona
89. Sindhi
90. Sinhala
91. Slovak
92. Slovenian
93. Somali
94. Spanish
95. Swahili
96. Swedish
97. Swiss
98. Tagalog
99. Tamazight
100. Tamil
101. Telugu
102. Thai
103. Tibetan
104. Turkish
105. Ukrainian
106. Urdu
107. Uzbeki
108. Vietnamese
109. Welsh
110. Xhosa
111. Yiddish
112. Yoruba
113. Zulu

Europe

Asia & the South Pacific

he time. See our website **www.eurotalk.com** for latest releases.

Vocabulary Builder language list:

- American English
- Albanian
- Arabic
- Cantonese
- Croatian
- Danish
- Dutch
- English
- Finnish
- French
- German
- Greek
- Hawaiian
- Hebrew
- Hungarian
- Icelandic
- Irish
- Italian
- Japanese
- Mandarin
- Maltese
- Manx
- Norwegian
- Papiamento
- Polish
- Portuguese
- Romanian
- Russian
- Scots Gaelic
- Spanish
- Swedish
- Turkish
- Welsh

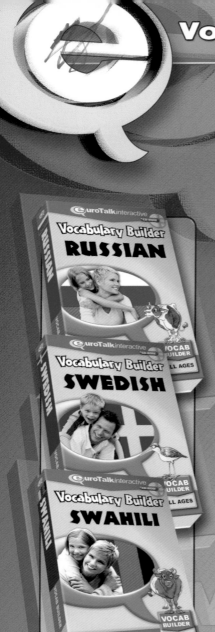

Learning new words really is **child's play** with this cartoon disc for **all ages**.

Language fun for all the family

THIS series is an ideal way to introduce languages to four to 12-year-olds. (Adults may enjoy it too.)

Vocabulary Builder's colourful cartoon pictures, which accompany each new word, immediately boost your memory power while its fun quizzes motivate you to remember what you've learnt, and a special recording feature checks your pronunciation.

Features include:
- A chance to record cartoons and play them back in your own "cinema".
- Nine games of varying difficulty, with points awarded for correct answers.
- More than 100 words, including colours, numbers, actions and simple sentences.
- A friendly tiger you can ask for help in your own language.

"A very slick disc, designed to teach vocabulary to children who have absolutely no knowledge of a foreign tongue."
The Guardian Education

Vocabulary Builder

Five dictionaries in One: English to and from French, German, Italian and Spanish

MORE than 2,000 words are spoken in five different languages to make this the essential dictionary for language learners.

Each of the dictionary entries includes the written word itself, an audio clip of how it's pronounced in your chosen language and a high quality picture or video clip of that word.

With a recording feature so you can compare your accent with the correct pronunciation, this is the perfect way to perfect your word power.

Special features include:

- Quizzes to help you remember what you've learnt. eg match the correct name to the picture.
- Fun work sheets that you can print out, fill in and use to test how much you've learnt.
- A printing facility so that you can have paper copies of the words and their translations (with or without pictures) to carry with you.

Asterix ®

Join in the riotous adventures of Asterix.

IF you are already competent in your new language and want to go to the next level, the Asterix CD-ROMs are for you.
The series, based on the adventures of the famous Gaul, help you to improve by watching an animated cartoon strip.
But, because the double CD-ROM pack is interactive, you are part of the action rather than the audience!

Special features:
- Dub over the leading characters with your own voice in the recording section.
- Select subtitles to the cartoon in a choice of languages.
- Ask "the professor" for help and handy tips on grammar.
- Use quizzes to test your understanding

Available in:
English
French
Spanish
German
Italian
Latin

Asterix ® & Picture Dictionary

Listen/Ecoutez 1&2

OUR Listen/Ecoutez! range brings traditional English or French language lessons to life for teenagers and adults.

There are two discs, Listen 1 and Listen 2, in the Learn English series and two discs, Ecoutez! 1 and Ecoutez! 2 in the Learn French series.

Each disc helps you to learn all the usual words you would be given in a classroom, with ten topics per disc. But, instead of having to study a list of vocabulary, you learn by listening to conversations that include the new words.

You are then asked questions about what you've heard, to check that you've understood and to win points for the correct answers.

10 Interactive English and French Lessons

Story World 1&2

Story World 1 and Story World 2 help youngsters from three-years-old upwards to learn English through play.

Children can watch a favourite illustrated story unfold on screen, then play games based on it. Helps youngsters to increase their vocabulary and improve their powers of concentration, while having fun at the same time.

A perfect way to introduce young children to computers. The Story World 1 disc features Goldilocks and the Three Bears, Three Billy Goats Gruff, Incy Wincy Spider and Humpty Dumpty.

The Story World 2 disc features Little Red Riding Hood, Jack and the Beanstalk, Hickory Dickory Dock and Jack and Jill.

English fun for Kids

Ecoutez/Listen & Story World

Audio CDs and DVD Videos

Audio CDs

TV and radio stars, including Felicity Kendall, Robert Powell and Sarah Miles, read world-famous literary classics. Choose from:
Rudyard Kipling's "Stories from the Jungle Book";
Kipling's "Just So Stories";
Oscar Wilde's "The Happy Prince" and other stories;
Hans Christian Andersen's "The Ugly Duckling" and other stories;
Edward Lear's "Nonsense Songs";
Katherine Mansfield's "Bliss" and other stories

Interactive DVD Videos

Interactive Cookery DVD Video
OUR "Interactive Thai Cooking DVD" takes you to the heart of South East Asia. It allows you to travel around Thailand, meet local chefs and gives you step-by-step instructions on how to follow their recipes.

Tourism DVD Video
OUR Insider Guide to London opens the door to the best attractions of the UK's capital city. As well as the world famous sights, it shows you the less well-known places that Londoners themselves would want to visit.

How To Order

OUR products are available from leading computer software stockists who often have special promotional offers.

They are also available direct from EuroTalk's website www.eurotalk.com where you can see our entire range and place an order.

Alternatively telephone, fax or post your order using the contact details below.

Schools and Colleges

MORE than 1,500 schools and colleges already use EuroTalk's language learning software as part of their teaching programmes and they are ideal tools for students of all ages.

There are network versions of our titles, which allow teachers to continually assess students' progress as individual quiz scores are recorded alongside pupils' names.

For more information click on the education button on the homepage

We believe in our products. If, having tried one, you are not happy with it for any reason, you can return it for a full refund.

Our contact details are:

Website: www.eurotalk.com
E-mail: info@eurotalk.co.uk
Tel: +44 (0) 207 371 7711 (International)
Free Phone: 0800 018 8838 (UK only)
Fax: +44 (0) 207 371 7781
Address: EuroTalk, 315-317 New Kings Road, London SW6 4RF
(Cheques should be made payable to EuroTalk Ltd.)

Information

We believe there is no such thing as someone who is bad at languages — only someone who hasn't yet discovered the right way to learn.

What the papers say

"....you'll find you just can't drag yourself away - in short, you can't stop yourself learning."
What PC Magazine

"....the most entertaining CD-ROM language packages come from the publisher EuroTalk..."
South China Post

"....succeeds in both the entertainment and educational stakes..."
Personal Computer World

"....they are certainly addictive..."
The Times

www.eurotalk.com